ALSO BY JUDITH VIORST

POEMS

The Village Square
It's Hard to Be Hip Over Thirty and Other Tragedies
    of Married Life
People and Other Aggravations
If I Were in Charge of the World and Other Worries
Forever Fifty and Other Negotiations
Sad Underwear and Other Complications
Suddenly Sixty and Other Shocks of Later Life
I'm Too Young to Be Seventy and Other Delusions
Unexpectedly Eighty and Other Adaptations
Wait for Me and Other Poems About the Irritations
    and Consolations of a Long Marriage
What Are You Glad About? What Are You Mad About?
Nearing Ninety and Other Comedies of Late Life

CHILDREN'S BOOKS

Sunday Morning
I'll Fix Anthony
Try It Again, Sam
The Tenth Good Thing About Barney
Alexander and the Terrible, Horrible, No Good, Very Bad Day
My Mama Says There Aren't Any Zombies, Ghosts, Vampires,
    Creatures, Demons, Monsters, Fiends, Goblins, or Things
Rosie and Michael
Alexander, Who Used to Be Rich Last Sunday
The Good-bye Book

OTHER

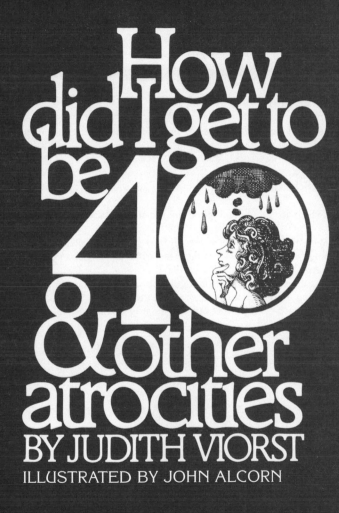

How did I get to be 40 & other atrocities

BY JUDITH VIORST

ILLUSTRATED BY JOHN ALCORN

Simon & Schuster

New York   London   Toronto   Sydney   New Delhi

Simon & Schuster
1230 Avenue of the Americas
New York, NY 10020

This Simon & Schuster hardcover edition April 2019

SIMON AND SCHUSTER and colophon are registered trademarks of Simon & Schuster, Inc.

For information about special discounts for bulk purchases, please contact Simon & Schuster Special Sales at 1-866-506-1949 or business@simonandschuster.com.

The Simon & Schuster Speakers Bureau can bring authors to your live event. For more information or to book an event, contact the Simon & Schuster Speakers Bureau at 1-866-248-3049 or visit our website at www.simonspeakers.com.

Illustrations by John Alcorn
Interior design by Herb Lubalin

Manufactured in the United States of America

10   9   8   7   6   5   4   3   2   1

Most of the poems appearing in this volume were originally published in *Redbook* magazine. "Twenty Questions" and "Some People's Children" first appeared in *New York* magazine.

Library of Congress Cataloging in Publication Data
Viorst, Judith
How did I get to be forty . . . and other atrocities.
1. Title
PS3572.16H6 811'.5'4 76-20546

ISBN 978-1-9821-2253-9
ISBN 978-1-5011-0588-3 (ebook)

For Joseph H. Smith and Phyllis Hersh

Contents

The truth is
If I had it all to do over
I still wouldn't study Swahili,
Learn to fly a plane,
Or take 92 lovers,
Some of them simultaneously.

The truth is
If I lived my life again
I still wouldn't leap before looking,
I still wouldn't count my chickens before they were hatched,
And I'd still, just in case I was hit by a car and had to be
        rushed to the hospital and examined,
Wear clean underwear.

The truth is
If I got a second chance
I still wouldn't know a forward pass from a backward one,
A self-effacing wine from a presumptuous one,
Or a man who, if I let him pick me up, would be rich, sincere,
        and of the same religious persuasion
From a man who, if I let him pick me up, would wind up being
        a homicidal rapist.

The truth is
That I'll always want to be
Pure enough to hate white bread,
Deep enough to admire Patagonian folk art.
Thin enough to go swimming in the nude,
Mature enough to outgrow Erich Fromm,
Nice enough to be nice to my Uncle Bernie,
And secure enough to not need getting married.

But the truth is
That the next time around,
I still wouldn't.

The sterilizer's up for grabs.
Nicked portacrib, good-bye.
My third and youngest son is growing older.
I'm done with dawn awakenings,
With pablum in my eye,
With small moist bundles burping on my shoulder.

I gave away my drawstring slacks
And smocks with floppy bows.
My silhouette will never more be pear-ish.
And though I'm left with stretch marks
And a few veins varicose,
I'm aiming for an image less ma-mère-ish.

No playpens in the living room
Will mangle my décor.
My stairs will not be blocked with safety fences.
No rattles, bottles, bibs, stuffed bears
Will disarray my floor,
No eau de diaper pail assail my senses.

And no more babies will disrupt
The tenor of my day,
Nor croup and teething interrupt my sleeping.
I swear to you I wouldn't have it
Any other way.
It's positively stupid to be weeping.

The Good Daughter

She's been a good daughter, my cousin Elaine
(In contrast to Walter her brother,
Who showed no respect). And she kept her room clean,
And she never talked fresh to her mother.
In college she tried, while maintaining straight A's,
To write twice a week or more often
(Unlike that bum Walter, who just called collect
And with news that drove nails in their coffin).

The boys Elaine went with were all that her folks
And their gin club and swim club expected.
(The girls Walter went with her folks only prayed
That he wouldn't come home from infected.)
Above-the-waist petting was all she allowed
Till the day she was led to the altar.
Yes, good is the word for my cousin Elaine.
(God knows what the word is for Walter.)

She's been a good daughter, my cousin Elaine,
As well as a good wife and mother.
She promised her folks that she's taking them in
When they're old. (Could they go with her brother?)
On how to raise children and which car to buy
She accepts their suggestions, and gladly.
(That Walter, believe me, you can't tell a thing.
He responds to advice very badly.)

Elaine, when a card should be sent, sends a card,
And a birthday is never forgotten.
(That Walter can't even remember the day
That his mother was born. Is that rotten?)
At forty Elaine can look back on a life
Where she followed the rules to the letter
And won the esteem of her mother and dad,
Except—they like Walter much better.

There Isn't a Thing to Worry About

What she does
Is
Wash oil off oily sea gulls, and
What he does
Is
Plant grass seed in the bare spots, so
Even though she's firm of flesh and
Barely out of her teens,
There isn't a thing to worry about,
I keep telling myself.

What she's into
Is
Zero population growth, and
What he's into
Is
Ace bandages, so
Even though he's thinking of buying
A pair of recycled jeans,
There isn't a thing to worry about,
I keep telling myself.

What she wants
Is
Everyone should love everyone, and
What he wants
Is
Low-interest home-improvement loans, so
Even though he spent the whole night singing
You've Got a Friend on the floor,
There isn't a thing to worry about,
I keep telling myself.

What she is
Is
Getting it all together, and
What he is
Is
Getting a little older, so
Even though he drove her home and
He should have been back around one and it's practically four,
There isn't a thing to worry about,
I keep telling myself,
I keep telling myself,
I keep telling myself.

Why do I care about looking good
When it's really my soul that counts?
Does Golda Meir feel diminished because of dry skin?
Why can't I give up my glosses and gels
And retain my superfluous hair,
And try to rely on what's known as the beauty within?

How come I think that the I that I am
Is enhanced by a shampoo and set?
Does Margaret Mead make herself crazy because of split ends?
And would she have run like a dummy to hide
In aisle nine of the Safeway last week
To avoid being seen with no eyeliner on by her friends?

Who would expect Madame Curie to tweeze?
Who would expect Joan of Arc
To go out and buy a new tunic before saving France?
I like to believe I'm a serious person
But sometimes my self-esteem rests
On whether there's more of my bottom than fits in my pants.

It's better, I know, to be loving and wise
Than merely size ten and unlined.
I mustn't forget where my ultimate value resides.
And surely a man like Paul Newman would want me
To have lots of beauty within.
But what could it hurt if I also looked gorgeous besides?

We've all turned into women with a matching set of luggage
and a butcher for our special cuts of meat,
And trouble getting to sleep if our room is too stuffy, too cold,
or not quiet enough, or the pillow is hard, or our sheet isn't
Tightly tucked in at the bottom.

And we've all turned into women with a standing hair appointment
and an air-conditioned car and name-brand bag,
And some drop-out Buddhist bisexual vegetarian Maoist children to
Aggravate us.

And we've all turned into women who know genuine in jewelry and
authentic in antiques and real in fur,
And the best in orthopedists for our frequently recurring
Lower back pain.

And we've all turned into women who take cabs instead of buses
and watch color, not the black and white, TV,
And have lawyers, gynecologists, accountants, dermatologists,
podiatrists, urologists, internists, cardiologists,
insurance agents, travel agents, brokers, ophthalmologists,
And no idea how we all turned into these women.

Among Other Thoughts on Our Wedding Anniversary

Over the years,
When the sink overflowed
Or the car ran out of gas
Or the lady who comes every Tuesday to clean didn't come
Or I felt pudgy
Or misunderstood
Or inferior to Marilyn Kaufman who is not only a pediatric
      surgeon but also a very fine person as well as beautiful
Or I fell in the creek and got soaked on our first family
      camping trip
Or mosquitoes ate me alive on our first family camping trip
Or I bruised my entire left side on our first family camping
      trip
Or I walked through a patch of what later turned out to be
      plenty of poison ivy on what later turned out to be our
      last family camping trip
Or my sweater shrank in the wash
Or I stepped on my glasses
Or the keys that I swear on my children's head I put on the
      top of the dresser weren't there
Or I felt depressed
Or unfulfilled
Or inferior to Ellen Jane Garver who not only teaches constitu-
      tional law but is also a wit plus sexually insatiable
Or they lost our luggage
Or our reservations
Or two of the engines
Or the rinse that was going to give my hair some subtle copper
      highlights turned it purple
Or my mother-in-law got insulted at something I said
Or my stomach got upset at something I ate
Or I backed into a truck that I swear when I looked in my
      rear-view mirror wasn't parked there
Or I suffered from some other blow of fate,
It's always been so nice to have my husband by my side so I could
Blame him.

What am I doing with a mid-life crisis?
This morning I was seventeen.
I have barely begun the beguine and it's
Good-night ladies
Already.

While I've been wondering who to be
When I grow up someday,
My acne has vanished away and it's
Sagging kneecaps
Already.

Why do I seem to remember Pearl Harbor?
Surely I must be too young.
When did the boys I once clung to
Start losing their hair?
Why can't I take barefoot walks in the park
Without giving my kidneys a chill?
There's poetry left in me still and it
Doesn't seem fair.

While I was thinking I was just a girl,
My future turned into my past.
The time for wild kisses goes fast and it's
Time for Sanka.
Already?

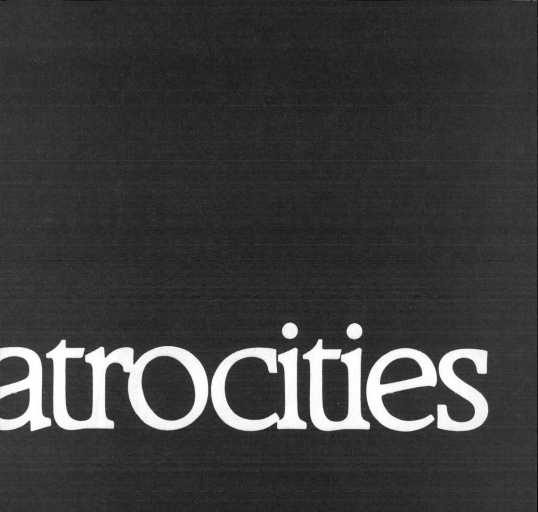

The Whole Truth

He always called her honey and
She always called him sweetie and
He always brought her flowers and
She always stroked his hair.
Their beautiful relationship was
What a marriage should be and
The rest of us regarded it with
Envy and despair.

She always called him lover and
He always called her baby and
She always praised his brilliance and
He always praised her wit.
No wife was more adoring and
No husband more devoted and
The rest of us were jealous I'm
Embarrassed to admit.

He always called her dearest and
She always called him darling and
He always hugged and kissed her and
She always held him tight.
They just announced they're filing for
Divorce tomorrow morning and
The news has filled the rest of us with
Absolute delight.

Leonard the Liberated Husband

Leonard the liberated husband,
Who was first on his block
With revolution,
Universal love,
Astrology,
Ecology,
And euthanasia,
Is finished with macho
And girlie magazines
And is currently
Washing dishes,
Waxing floors,
Relating to women as
Genuine human beings,
Deploring rape
And other oppressive conditions,
And insisting that his wife pursue
Personhood,
Ph.D.'s,
Sexual bliss,
Greater respect from truck drivers,
And highly paid executive positions.

Whether she wants to,
Or not.

Life isn't fair.
Many a meanie is happy, while
Certifiable saints are frequently sad, and
Cads have perfect digestion while honeys get gas pains.

Life isn't fair.
Planner-aheaders are rained on, while
People who never call Weather never have clouds, and
Loudmouths get service while gentle folks get soup stains.

And men with sensitive souls and big potbellies and
      wrinkles and gray
Often drive young women mad with lust,
While women with sensitive souls and big potbellies and
      wrinkles and gray
Often drive their husbands to the bus stop.

Life isn't fair.
Virgins get zircons and vinyl, while
Wicked wild wantons wind up with the diamonds and mink, and
Thinkers get headaches while dummies get admired.

Life isn't fair.
Worriers wind up in traction, while
Live-and-let-livers are rarely assaulted by fate, and
Late birds get worms while early birds get tired.

And virtue isn't rewarded and the meek don't inherit
      the earth
And truth does not prevail and justice is flawed.
And mothers and fathers with master's degrees have
      harpsichord tuners for sons
And bad guys finish first while nice guys get audits.

Life isn't fair.
Some folks stay fat drinking Fresca, while
Others who only drink malteds keep staying thin, and
Cynics survive while babes in the woods don't make it.

Life isn't fair.
Those who don't water have roses, while
Sprayers and pruners and weeders wind up having blight, and
I might take exception, if only I knew where to take it.

Secret Meetings

Ellie and Marvin
Have been having secret meetings twice a week
For the past six months
But have thus far failed to consummate
Their passion
Because
While both of them agree
That marital fidelity
Is not only unrealistic but also
Irrelevant,

She has developed migraines, and
He has developed these sharp shooting pains
In his chest, and
She's got impetigo, and
He's got pinkeye.

Ellie and Marvin
Drive forty miles to sneaky luncheonettes
In separate cars
But have thus far done no more than
Heavy necking
Because
While both of them agree
That sexual exclusivity
Is not only adolescent but also
Retrograde,
She has developed colitis, and
He has developed these dull throbbing pains
In his back, and
She's started biting her nails, and
He's smoking again.

Ellie and Marvin
Yearn to have some love in the afternoon
At a motor hotel
But have thus far only had a lot of
Coffee
Because
He is convinced that his phone is being tapped, and
She is convinced that a man in a trench coat is following her, and
He says what if the motor hotel catches fire, and
She says what if she talks some night in her sleep, and
She thinks her husband is acting suspiciously hostile, and
He thinks his wife is acting suspiciously nice, and
He keeps cutting his face with his double-edge razor, and
She keeps closing her hand in the door of her car, so
While both of them agree
That guilt is not only neurotic but also
Obsolete,
They've also agreed
To give up
Secret meetings.

Some people's children
Have always known a starboard from a port
And that inchoate without the in
Is not the way a person pronounces Choate
and
Some people's children
Are never anything less than the III or the IV
And enter life equipped with
A mummy, a nanny, good bones, a private income, and
     all the right friends and labels in their coats
and
Some people's children
Always marry girls named Whitney Cartwright
Or Cartwright Whitney
And never marry girls named Charmaine Glitz
but
Even if our children went to Harvard and joined racquet clubs
And summered in Newport and wintered at St. Moritz
And no longer took off their shoes and their socks in
     the living room
In order to scratch the bottom of their feet
And turned into ambassadors and bankers and Republicans
And gave up trying to talk and eat at the same time
and
Even if they learned which things that, no matter how much
     they liked them, they shouldn't admit it
and
Even if they learned which things that, no matter how much
     they didn't like them, they should
and
Even if they acquired the finest in elocution and riding boots
     and tailors
You still would never mistake them for
Some people's children.

Eating My Heart Out

Beethoven, deaf and unlucky in love,
Sat himself down to compose.
Van Gogh, feeling rather depressed,
Was impelled to paint pictures.
But when I'm sad I'm also
Bulging out of all my clothes
From eating everything except the fixtures.

Misery makes a pig of me.
Ennobled I am not.
Somehow I only get famished
While others get finer.
Misery offers food for thought,
But food's the thought I've got.
And I'm searching, instead of my soul,
For an all-night diner.

I'd gladly settle for sleepless nights.
I'd settle for black despair.
I'd settle for quietly weeping
In neighborhood bars.
But when I get unhappy
I don't merely tear my hair.
I tear into three dozen Mallomars.

Misery makes some people deep.
It always makes me wide.
My breast and a pint of whipping cream
I'm beating.
Misery makes some people grow.
I grow from side to side.
My heart out isn't the only thing
That I'm eating.

Why can't I just have fainting spells,
Or touchingly haunted eyes?
Why not a pitiful pallor,
Or trembling lips?
Why must sorrow visit me
With cravings for peach pies
And fourteen extra pounds around the hips?

Misery knocks me off my feet,
But never off my feed.
And the lump in my throat is concealed
By my double chin.
Misery piques my appetite.
Such help I didn't need.
I only wish that happiness
Made me thin.

Open House

Everyone is coming to our party,
Everyone, that is, except the Stones,
Who stopped being the Stones when she started saying that
      the trouble with America was the CIA and the FBI and
      the exploitation of lettuce growers and Indians, and
He started saying the trouble was not enough tennis courts, but
Everyone else is coming to our party,
Everyone, that is, except the Hoyts,
Who stopped being the Hoyts when they started saying that
      just because a husband and wife are sexually unfaithful
      doesn't mean that they're being unfaithful emotionally, but
Everyone else is coming to our party,
Everyone, that is, except the Kings,
Who stopped being the Kings when she decided that
      every time she told him something sensitive and deep
      he didn't get it, and
He decided that every time he told her something funny
      she didn't get it, but
Everyone else is coming to our party,
Everyone, that is, except the Youngs,
Who stopped being the Youngs when she started law school,
And he started saying the house is never clean,
And she started saying why don't you clean it yourself,
And he started saying that women should clean and
      men should go to law school, but
Everyone else is coming to our party,
Everyone, that is, except the Clarks,
Who stopped being the Clarks when she decided to seek inner peace
      through wheat germ and meditation, and
He decided to seek inner peace through Gay Lib, but
Everyone else is coming to our party,
Everyone, that is, except the Greens,
Who stopped being the Greens when they sold their house and
      moved to the country to rediscover each other, and re-
      discovered they didn't agree about garlic. Or Woody Allen.
      Or Scrabble, her father, cloth napkins, or psychoanalysis.
      Or when is the music so loud that it's giving you headaches.
      Or when is a room so ice-cold that your fingers get numb, but
Everyone else is coming to our party.
I hope we'll be there.

Three in
the Morning

At three in the morning I used to be sleeping an untroubled
       sleep in my bed,
But lately at three in the morning I'm tossing and turning,
Awakened by hypochondria, and gas, and nameless dread,
Whose name I've been learning.

At three in the morning I brood about what my cholesterol count
       might reveal,
And the pains in my chest start progressing from gentle to racking,
While certain intestinal problems make clear that the onions I ate
       with my meal
Plan on counterattacking.

At three in the morning I reach for the bottle of pills that
       I seem to possess
Increasingly larger amounts of as every year passes,
Except that I can't tell the ones for my nerves from the ones
       for my stomach distress
Till I put on my glasses.

At three in the morning I look toward the future with blankets
       pulled over my ears,
And all of my basic equipment distinctly diminished.
My gums are receding, my blood pressure's high, and I can't begin
       listing my fears
Or I'll never get finished.

At three in the morning I used to be sleeping but lately I wake
       and reflect
That my girlhood has gone and I'll now have to manage without it.
They tell me that I'm heading into my prime. From the previews
       I do not expect
To be crazy about it.

I made him swear he'd always tell me nothing but the truth.
I promised him I never would resent it,
No matter how unbearable, how harsh, how cruel. How come
He thought I meant it?

The Sensuous Woman

I'm giving up nice and becoming a sensuous woman,
The kind of a woman who wouldn't wear bedsocks to bed.
I'm giving up going to places like Saks and the cleaners
And going wherever my appetites lead me instead.
I've bought all these books that are teaching me how to
        discover
Erogenous zones that would make my Aunt Ida drop dead.
And as soon as I've found them, I'll go be
A sensuous woman.

I'm giving up good and becoming a seething inferno,
One of those forces of nature mere mortals can't tame.
Beneath my beige knit (polyester) such cravings will smolder
That Uncle Jerome, if he heard, would pass out from the shame.
The books say that even a middle-class girl from New Jersey
Can fan, if she practices, practically anyone's flame.
And as soon as I've practiced, I'll go be
A seething inferno.

I'm giving up sweet and becoming a creature of passion,
A wild thing that nobody ever can fully possess.
I'm leaving behind me a lot of wrecked lives, plus some
        heartache.
(You think that a creature of passion would settle for less?)
My cousin Elaine, let me tell you, does not even know from
The animal needs that the books say I need to express.
And as soon as I need them, I'll go be
A creature of passion.

I'm giving up G and becoming an X-rated woman,
With black satin sheets and an overhead mirror or two.
I've still got some years, between car pools and Medicare
        payments,
To do all those things I've been warned all my life not to do.
The books say I'll learn to stop worrying what my Aunt Ida
And Uncle Jerome, and my mother, would think if they knew.
And as soon as I've stopped, I will go be
A sensuous woman.

I have grown to understand that
People whose accents are British
May not be smarter than people whose accents are Bronx,
But British helps, and that
Peace of mind is more to be treasured than rubies,
But trust funds help, and that
While it's better to die on your feet than to live on your knees,
What about stooping?

I have grown to understand that
People whose best friends are rock stars
Often are duller than people whose best friends are us,
But rock stars help, and that
Inner satisfaction counts more than approval,
But clapping helps, and that
While it's better to light a candle than curse the darkness,
First you could curse.

I have grown to understand that
People whose fathers adored them
Feel just as jumpy as people whose fathers said feh,
But love helps, and that
Self-reliance is braver than being dependent,
But help helps, and that
While it's better, as everyone knows, to give than receive,
Nobody says that you always have to be
Better.

I've finished six pillows in Needlepoint,
And I'm reading Jane Austen and Kant,
And I'm up to the pork with black beans in Advanced Chinese Cooking.
I don't have to struggle to find myself
For I already know what I want.
I want to be healthy and wise and extremely good-looking.

I'm learning new glazes in Pottery Class,
And I'm playing new chords in Guitar,
And in Yoga I'm starting to master the lotus position.
I don't have to ponder priorities
For I already know what they are:
To be good-looking, healthy, and wise.
And adored in addition.

I'm improving my serve with a tennis pro,
And I'm practicing verb forms in Greek,
And in Primal Scream Therapy all my frustrations are vented.
I don't have to ask what I'm searching for
Since I already know that I seek
To be good-looking, healthy, and wise.
And adored.
And contented.

I've bloomed in Organic Gardening,
And in Dance I have tightened my thighs,
And in Consciousness Raising there's no one around who can top me.
And I'm working all day and I'm working all night
To be good-looking, healthy, and wise.
And adored.
And contented.
And brave.
And well-read.
And a marvelous hostess,
Fantastic in bed,
And bilingual,
Athletic,
Artistic ...
Won't someone please stop me?

Another Wife's Husband

I could be such a wonderful wife to another wife's husband,
To someone who isn't aware that I bleach my moustache,
That strawberries give me a rash, that what I've got
Instead of muscle tone is insomnia.

I wouldn't let on that I rarely choose calm over panic,
Or suffer in silence if offered a chance to complain,
That I tend to collapse under strain, that what I lack
In nerve I'm making up in anxiety.

He wouldn't find out that I sometimes still count on my fingers.
He wouldn't find out I'm not nearly as clean as I'm neat,
That my hair frizzes up in the heat, that what I'm better
At holding than tennis racquets are grudges.

With him I'd get more into lust and less into housework.
With him I'd be plucky and jaunty and wonderfully warm,
And I'd keep all illusion intact. It's the kind of unnatural act
That only another wife's husband could make me perform.

Twenty Questions

Can a person who used to wear a Ban the Bomb button
And a Free Angela Davis button
And an Uppity Women Unite button
And a Get Out of Viet Nam button
Find happiness being a person with a
Set of fondue forks, a fish poacher, and a wok?

Is there an economic rule that says
No matter how much we earn and how little we spend,
There's no such thing as getting out of hock?

How do I know if the time has come to
Accept my limitations,
Or whether I still ought to try to
Fulfill my promise?

How come I'm reading articles
With names like A Woman's Guide to Cosmetic Surgery
More than I'm reading the poems of Dylan Thomas?

If I had an either/or choice
Would I prefer to be deservedly respected,
Or would I prefer to be mindlessly adored?

If we totally take the blame when our children
Stutter and wet their beds,
And are busted and maladjusted and drop out of school,
Do we get to take the credit if our children
Grow up to be brilliant, plus very nice people,
Plus mentally healthy and chairmen of the board?

When, instead of vice versa,
Did I start to pick investments over adventure,
And clean over scenic, and comfortable over intense?

Why does a relationship
Between an older woman and younger man
Suddenly seem to make a lot of sense?

Why am I always buying the clothes which,
When they first come out,
Nothing on earth (I swear) could make me buy?

What are the things which,
Even though people won't be upset (they swear)
If I'll only admit,
I should always deny?

Are some human beings
Intellectually and emotionally incapable
Of ever reading a road map,
Or could I still learn to?

If six days a week I'm responsible
And self-sufficient and competent and mature,
On the seventh could I go find a womb to return to?

Couldn't a person who isn't expecting
Praise for what she's doing
At least expect some praise for not expecting it?

If I think that the fellow next door
Is attempting to give me a kiss in the kitchen,
Am I first allowed to be kissed before rejecting it?

How can I learn to relate to marijuana
And bisexuality
When I'm more at home with The Anniversary Waltz?

How come I've got these incredible insights
Into all of my faults,
And I've still got my faults?

Why couldn't somebody tell me
That I haven't changed since college
Without being practically blind or
A terrible liar?

Why, since I've never had any intention
Of going out on the streets and selling my body,
Is it hard to be reaching an age where
I won't find a buyer?

How come a charter member of NOW
Is afraid to confess to her husband
That the first day she drove their new car
She dented the fender?

How will I ever be able to tell
If what I achieve in life
Ought to be called serenity — not surrender?

Alone I could own both sides of the double bed
And stay up reading novels half the night.
And no one would be here telling me turn off the light
And hogging the blankets.

And no one would be here saying he's taking the car
And noticing that I let the milk turn sour.
Alone I could talk long distance for an hour
And who would stop me?

Alone a hard-boiled egg could be a meal
And the living-room couch could be red, not compromise-green.
And no one would be here making me go to Queens
For family brunches.

And no one would be here brushing his teeth with my brush
And pushing the thermostat down to sixty degrees.
Alone I could give Goodwill my boots and my skis
And switch to beaches.

Alone I could give up understanding Brie,
Détente, the Superbowl, and Cousin Rose.
And no one would be here telling me which of my clothes
Make me look chunky.

And no one would be here steaming the bathroom up
And wanting his back massaged and his buttons sewn.
And no one would be here. I would be alone.
And I would hate it.

I'm facing the fact that
I'll never write Dante's Inferno
Or paint a Picasso
Or transplant a kidney or build
An empire, nor will I ever
Run Israel or Harvard,
Appear on the cover of Time,
Star on Broadway, be killed
By a firing squad for some noble ideal,
Find the answer
To racial injustice or whether God's dead
Or the source
Of human unhappiness,
Alter the theories of Drs.
S. Freud, C. G. Jung, or A. Einstein,
Or maybe the course
Of history,
In addition to which
I am facing the fact that
I'll never compose Bach cantatas,
Design Saint Laurents,
Advise presidents, head U.S. Steel,
Resolve the Mideast,
Be the hostess of some major talk show,
Or cure the cold,
And although future years may reveal
Some hidden potential,
Some truly magnificent act that
I've yet to perform,
Or some glorious song to be sung
For which I'll win prizes and praise,
I must still face the fact that
They'll never be able to say,
"And she did it so young."

More from bestselling author
JUDITH VIORST